# Contents

CW01499033

# Tackle Gymnastics

*Also by Nik Stuart*
Gymnastics for Men

# Tackle Gymnastics

Nik Stuart and
Alan Sommerville

Stanley Paul

London Melbourne Sydney Auckland Johannesburg

Stanley Paul & Co. Ltd

An imprint of the Hutchinson Publishing Group

3 Fitzroy Square, London W1P 6JD

Hutchinson Group (Australia) Pty Ltd
30-32 Cremorne Street, Richmond South, Victoria 3121
PO Box 151, Broadway, New South Wales 2007

Hutchinson Group (NZ) Ltd
32-34 View Road, PO Box 40-086, Glenfield, Auckland 10

Hutchinson Group (SA) (Pty) Ltd
PO Box 337, Bergvlei 2012, South Africa

First published 1980
© Nik Stuart and Alan Sommerville 1980

Set in Monophoto Times by Tradespools Ltd, Frome, Somerset

Printed in Great Britain by The Anchor Press Ltd
and bound by Wm Brendon & Son Ltd
both of Tiptree, Essex

ISBN 0 09 139310 8 (cased)
0 09 139311 6 (paper)

# Preface

The successful development of the gymnast comes about through a close working relationship between gymnasts on the one hand and the teacher or coach on the other. The techniques of modern Olympic gymnastics can only be understood properly through a study of the physical and mechanical principles on which they are based. In explaining these principles, the text is often, of necessity, fairly technical. The young gymnast should not be put off by this, since these parts of the book are intended for the teacher or coach, who will be able to interpret and explain the relevant information.

Although scientific exposition is followed where possible by a simplified synopsis, the young gymnast will gain most from the diagrams and photographs showing the step by step progressions, and the descriptions accompanying them.

Although much of the preparation work shown at the end of the first chapter may be done quite safely at home, the gymnast is advised only to practise the skills under the supervision of the teacher or coach.

# Introduction

The sport of artistic gymnastics has grown so fast over the last few years that many of the new and revolutionary ideas on coaching and performing have not yet had time to reach the millions of girls and boys now practising this most demanding of sports.

In this book we try to provide some of the up to date techniques and philosophies applied to the basic elements so that the would-be champions will have a sound base on which to build the more difficult skills in the future.

The road to the top is long and hard work all the way, but there are rewards at all levels of participation. Besides badges and certificates the most worthwhile reward is the satisfaction of success. The coach's job is to ensure that success is a regular part of the gymnast's development and this will only happen if both pupil and teacher have an understanding of their responsibilities.

The road to the top starts for most young gymnasts in the school gymnastic classes and gym clubs. Here they will learn the basic movements and hopefully the exercises that will prepare them for more difficult skills. The schools, however, must cater for a wide range of activities and often are not able to take spare time for specialized coaching. School teachers may advise the talented gymnast to join a club, where they will be able to practise several times a week under expert coaches.

Many of the new sports and leisure centres are now running gymnastic classes for children and often have their own resident clubs. Gymnastics has become so popular that most clubs have a waiting list and entrance test to select only the best and most talented boys and girls. The following chapter will tell you about the way in which selection is made and what the coaches are looking for in the potential champion.

Once in an established gymnastics club the hard work starts in earnest, and a rigorous programme is needed to take the gymnast from competition and trial to club team, county team, regional team and eventually to national team.

Hard work and dedication are essential at club level, but above all the gymnast must be prepared to listen carefully and accept the coach's instructions. If you are not succeeding, it is probably because you are not following the coach's advice, and even more probably because you have not been following the coach's advice with regard to your preparation work.

# 1 Preparation
## The key to success

In many sports it is possible to participate with a certain amount of success almost at once. Nearly everyone could kick, throw or hit a ball, for instance, in the first few attempts without problems. These actions are within the capacity of our bodies, without any special training. In gymnastics, however, even the most basic moves are beyond the normal physical capacity of most people, without special training.

How many people do you know who are not trained gymnasts who can take their weight on their arms in a handstand, or can show a 'splits' position? Not many, and this is because in normal everyday life the human body does not need these special requirements of strength and suppleness.

Every movement and skill in gymnastics has its own special requirements of preparation in the following areas:

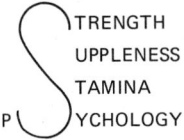

TRENGTH

UPPLENESS

TAMINA

P    YCHOLOGY

Once the necessary preparation work has been done in each of these Ss of gymnastics, the learning of the skills is easy. Many gymnasts and coaches become frustrated through trying skills which they have not prepared for properly in one or more of these areas, often wrongly blaming the student's inability to learn.

*Preparation + Knowledge + Coaching = SUCCESS*

*What* then are we looking for in each of these areas, and *how* can we achieve our aims?

## Mobility

Mobility or suppleness (the range of movement in a joint) is necessary so that the correct techniques can be used in the learning of skills. Besides allowing proper use of the scientific principles of mechanics, full range of movement has an aesthetic quality enhancing all performance.

Full mobility should be attained before the skills are learnt, since skills will be mastered much more easily with correct technique and will tend to perpetuate the particular range of movement thereafter.

The handspring provides a good example of the need for full range of movement in the splits position. In the handspring the front leg needs to thrust until the back leg has swung through handstand (Figure 1a). If the gymnast has a poor splits the swinging back leg will pull the thrusting front leg off the floor before it has finished pushing (Figure 1b) and the resulting handspring will be low.

Figure 1

There are many factors which limit the range of movement in a joint, but for all practical purposes there are only two factors that we can significantly alter:

## 1 *The muscles and muscle sheaths*

These are probably the main limiters of movement and provide one area in which we can bring about change. Our aim in this area is to make the muscles relax completely. As far as is known, muscle fibres will not stretch, they can only be encouraged to relax.

## 2 *The myotatic reflex*

This is a reflex action in muscles which exists to protect the muscle from damage. In very simple terms the myotatic reflex comes into operation in violent and rapid exertions of the muscle. If, for example, you were trying to increase your splits by standing, holding a support and swinging your leg violently as high as possible, the sensors in the muscle would send a message to the brain to say that you were likely to do damage. Without your being aware of this, the brain would send a message back to the muscle telling it to resist. Your attempt to increase your mobility would be frustrated without your knowing about it.

### *How does one increase range of movement?*

1 Something is required to help the muscle to relax.
2 Something is required to help suppress the myotatic reflex.
3 Something is required to take the body part a little further than its previous range of movement or habit length.

For point 1 a way of heating and warming up the muscle is required. The most usual way is by active heating through some form of activity like running and jumping in a game.

If this method is used it is important to insulate the body well with warm clothing; track suits are ideal but the extremities should not be forgotten and hats, gloves and warm socks should be included. How often I have seen the warm-up wasted, by youngsters discarding all their warm clothing after the exercises, allowing the heat to leave their bodies as they settle down to the suppling session.

The disadvantage of active heating is that it may be exhausting, especially in cold weather, thereby cutting down the effectiveness of later work in the session.

Another way of heating the body which is particularly effective and suitable for the 'at home' suppling sessions, is passive heating in the form of a hot bath or shower. This is followed by a quick towelling down and then into warm insulating clothing. This method has three advantages: it requires little physical effort, it is very relaxing, and at once the muscles and joints are heated to a higher temperature.

Now to points 2 and 3 which are dealt with together because for this purpose they are interrelated. Slow passive movements are recommended for all mobility exercises since they do not provoke the myotatic reflex, together with a prolonged relaxation in which some external force in the form of gravity or a partner is used to extend the body part beyond its normal range or habit length.

Finally, the gymnast should try to incorporate any increase of range of movement into the technique of his skills so that any improvement is maintained. In many skills a definite improvement will be noticed as mobility increases and indeed the degree of suppleness can often be the deciding factor between success and failure.

Suppleness is an innate factor in the first place, and some fortunate individuals are born with long habit lengths in their muscles. For many, however, suppling exercises are a continuing and necessary part of the gymnast's work programme.

**How to improve range of movement – step by step**

1 *Warm the limbs* involved either by activity or by a hot bath or shower. Insulate the body well, including head, hands and feet; this will minimize the amount of exercise necessary to get warm.
2 *Keep warm* by continuing to insulate the body during the exercise.
3 *Extend the body* parts beyond their normal 'habit length' using some external force. Maintain a slow steady pressure and relax as much as possible for about 30 seconds in each exercise.
4 *Repeat the exercises daily.* Regular sessions often are far more valuable than one hard session now and again.
5 *Use* your increased range of movement in your gymnastic skills.

**Strength and stamina**

Before looking at how to increase strength and stamina let us first arrive at a working definition of these words:

STRENGTH – Strength can be thought of as the muscular force required to move a given weight through a given distance. An example is pushing from headstand to handstand; to be strong enough to do this the muscles of the arms and shoulders must exert enough force to move the mass of the body against the opposition of gravity, through the distance of the extending arms (Figure 2a and b).

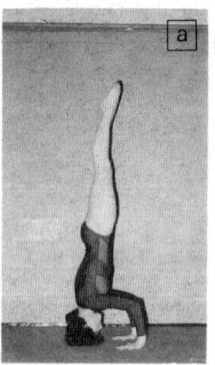

Figure 2   *(left)*

Figure 3   *(opposite)*
The crucifix on rings

STAMINA – If we can perform a given exercise once we are strong enough to do the move, and if we wish to perform the same move many times, the muscles involved must develop local endurance or stamina. Using the previous example, to push to handstand once is a measure of strength, to do so repeatedly is a measure of endurance or stamina.

Another factor affecting both strength and stamina is *time*. When we move the body mass through a distance very quickly we are generating what is known as explosive strength or power, while to repeat an exercise many times in a short time involves more endurance than when the muscles are given time to recover a little after each exercise.

It can be seen then that there are many different forms of strength and stamina and every movement in artistic gymnastics requires a special combination of muscular strength, stamina and power, involving its own particular muscles in differing sequence and combinations, though many movements have strength and stamina factors in common.

Figure 4  Example of 'explosive' strength

Figure 5   Swinging the straight body round the pommel horse needs great stamina

In men's gymnastics, the crucifix on rings (Figure 3), shows strength used to keep the body static against the force of gravity; this is known as isometric strength.

In the headspring (Figure 4) the rapid straightening of the thrusting arms and shoulder and rapid extension of the body from piked to straight are examples of 'explosive' strength or power.

Also in men's gymnastics, the swinging of the straight body around the pommel horse (Figure 5), while in support, involves great muscular endurance or stamina.

How can strength and stamina be increased? The very practice of gymnastic skills will necessarily increase strength, but the process will be slow and frustrating.

If, for example, the would-be gymnast wishes to learn the handspring and tries to do so without first developing the necessary arm and shoulder strength to support the body weight, the gymnast will, for a period of months, perform the move with bent arms, poor technique and possible headaches, as he crashes, nose first, into the ground. Gradually, the necessary strength will be developed to avoid injury, but the bad habits gained will be most difficult to lose.

The wise gymnast will decide which areas need strengthening, devise exercises in isolation from the skill, and practise until all the necessary areas are improved to the degree where the skill can be attempted confidently.

Great care must be taken in devising exercises to increase strength and stamina since they are specific to each gymnastic skill, e.g. doing press-ups will not make one stronger or give more stamina, except in the press-up position, and will be of no use in increasing strength in handstand, for instance.

Expert and detailed knowledge are necessary for strength training, and young gymnasts must consult with their coaches before using aids like weights or elastic strands, since serious injury can result from misuse of this equipment. However, there are many worthwhile exercises which can be done using the body's own weight as a resistance and the general rules are as follows.

The body is a very efficient machine and will only work when necessary. The increase of strength and stamina involve the body in having to do quite a lot of extra work. Firstly, the muscle is made up of hundreds of thousands of individual fibres, many of which do no work. These lazy fibres have to be woken up and made to work by increased nervous stimulation. Secondly, if the muscle has more active fibres it needs more food from the blood. The body, therefore, has to increase the blood supply to and from the muscle to bring in more oxygen and carry away the extra waste products. Small wonder then that the body will only increase strength when absolutely necessary. To the body, necessity constitutes stress. This means that, unless the muscle is pulled beyond its normal expected work load, the body will take no action.

The principle involved is called the progressive overload principle – pushing or overloading the muscles repeatedly so that the body takes the hint. Unfortunately, the body has a safety mechanism in the form of discomfort and pain so that overloading exercise involves working beyond comfort, but not into the pain barrier. Different people have differing thresholds of pain which inevitably causes different work rates and progress rates.

**How to improve strength – step by step**

1 *Warm up* the muscles as for suppling to avoid damage through tears and strains.
2 Make the exercises specific and relate exactly to their function in the gymnastic skill.

3 Progressively overload the muscles – always try to do a little more than last time, e.g. a bit more resistance or a few more repetitions.
4 Push yourself beyond comfort but not into pain.
5 Monitor your progress and keep records in a training diary. This will help to motivate you, and be patient – the body will take a while to respond.
6 Devise your own exercises to meet the requirements of your specific stage of development and, in general, never train for strength and stamina before a skill session.
7 Don't use apparatus or weights without the supervision of your coach.

To summarize, the gymnast needs to prepare his or her body in various ways before attempting the skills. The areas of preparation are: range of movement, strength, and endurance. Using an example we can see how these are related.

Let us take, as an example, the splits. This is a lateral extension of the pelvic girdle with right or left leg forwards. By following a programme of daily exercise, using the correct methods, full range of movement is eventually acquired. At the same time as the range of movement is developing, we should be aiming to develop strength and stamina within the range. Many supple young gymnasts will show a perfect splits position while on the floor, showing they have the full range of movement potential; when asked to hang from a bar and lift the legs into splits, or to stand and raise the legs against gravity, they show a decided lack of strength and stamina.

*Failure to meet the requirements in any of the areas of preparation will frustrate the learning process.*

**Psychology**

By psychology I mean the gymnast's attitude of mind. This requires preparation and development in the same way as the physical factors.

Motivation is more important than all the physical factors for, if the gymnast has the ideal physique but lacks the basic desire to be a good gymnast, the rest is worthless. Whereas a strongly motivated gymnast can overcome almost any physical problem eventually.

The motivating factors can be many and varied, but are usually composite. A gymnast may work to please a parent, the coach, the teacher; to be part of a group; to participate with friends; to compete; to prove himself or herself, and for many other reasons. No matter what the first motivating factors are, the individual must eventually get sufficient reward from the sport to encourage further participation.

Starts with the need to be a gymnast

Good preparation leads to confidence and progressive success which satisfies and motivates further preparation etc. The magic word, however, is *preparation* – the greater the work put in at this point, the greater will be the rewards, and the stronger the motivation to further efforts.

**The preparation exercises**

The following pages of exercises are a guide to provide a good basic vocabulary of physical preparation. As progress is made to more difficult skills, particular emphasis will be necessary in one or more of these areas or in specific areas not shown.

The exercises are set out in general groups for different parts of the body. As suppleness improves through a given range of movement, strength and stamina must be increased within the same range of movement since all three factors together make up the total preparation. The exercises included are only intended to provide a basic vocabulary of preparation. Each new skill to be learnt will have its own special individual requirements in each area of preparation and the exercises will need to be modified and increased as the gymnast progresses. Do not expect instant results. A half an hour's practice every day is far more beneficial than a heavy session once a week. Have patience and results will soon be noticed. Always follow the general rules laid out below.

*Suppleness*
1 Always warm up first (games or a hot bath or shower).
2 Keep warm by insulating with suitable clothing (don't forget hands, feet and head).
3 Move into position slowly and try to relax beyond the normal habit length.
4 Hold each position for 30 seconds while relaxing.
5 Repeat each practice three times.

*Strength*
1 Warm up.
2 Keep warm.
3 Use good form and style while practising.

4 Repeat the exercises ten times each *or* build up to ten.
5 When ten repetitions are reached increase the speed of work.

*Stamina*
1 Warm up.
2 Keep warm.
3 Always maintain good form and style.
4 Repeat the exercise as many times as you can, remembering to put up with discomfort, but not pain.
5 Add one repetition to your previous day's score each time, up to a maximum of fifty.

The exercises are grouped together related to the different body parts, e.g. the trunk section contains range of movement exercises and the allied strength and stamina work. Work through each section, or choose one exercise from each section on a rota basis.

It is much more beneficial to work with a friend or helpful coach or parent, so that the elements of competition and companionship prevent the exercises from becoming boring.

# The Preparation
## Exercises

**Trunk**
Suppleness

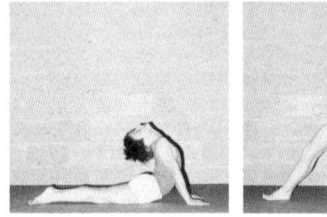

Strength

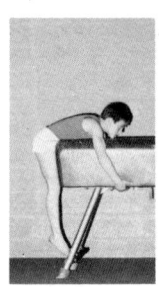

Stamina

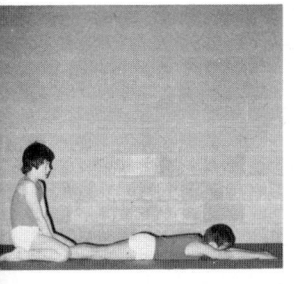
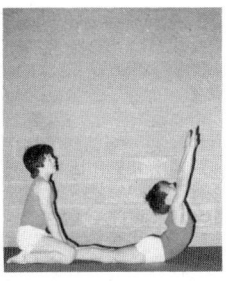

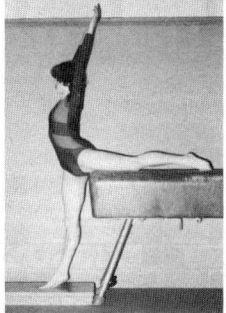

**Lumbar**
Supple-
ness

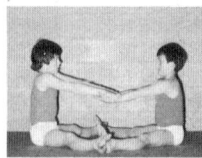 

Strength

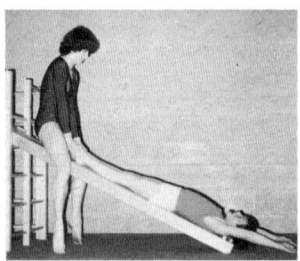 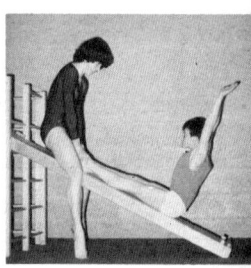

Stamina

 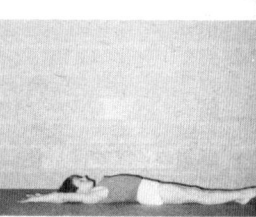

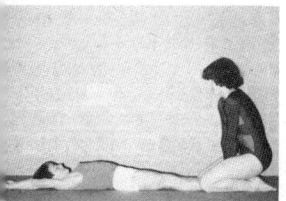

**Legs**
Suppleness

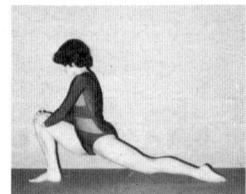

Strength

Stamina

**Shoulders**
Suppleness

 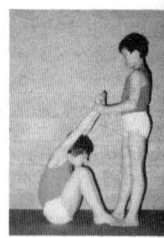

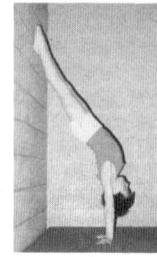 

 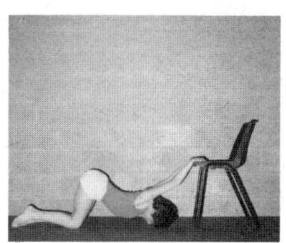

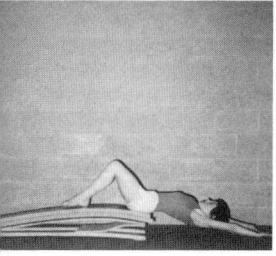 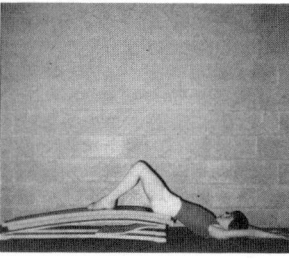

Some other useful exercises
for strength and stamina

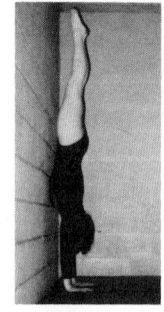 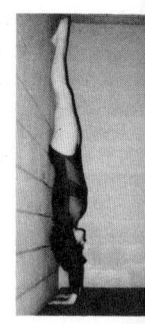

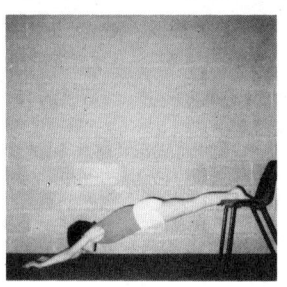 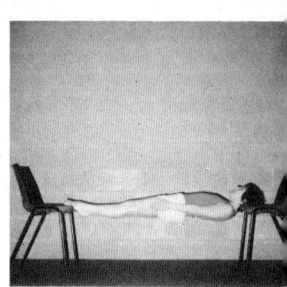

# 2 Floor exercises
## Basic skills

### Skill

Before looking at the basic skill of the sport, we should have a clear idea of what we mean by the word 'skill'.

A skill in gymnastics terms is performing a given muscular sequence with precise control, making optimum use of strength, range of movement and mechanical principles.

A skill should be subject to conscious control and in this respect differs from a 'habit' which is an automatic response to a given stimulus.

If we have mastered the handspring as a skill, eventually, through repetition, we can perform the element without conscious control – it has become a habit.

Now the habit comes about by constant repetition and once formed is hard to alter. Many gymnasts practise very hard at producing bad habits simply because they are not aware that the habit-making process is in progress.

As an example let us continue with the handspring, which a girl gymnast has learnt to perfection. The gymnast knows that, when she concentrates, she will perform her handspring with perfect style – legs straight, arms extended, toes pointed, etc. However, in most of her training, she does not concentrate so hard and gradually the details are allowed to relax. Every time she practises the handspring without perfect form she is changing the skill into a habit by repeating the imperfection. The gymnast remains confident, however, that when she wishes to she will still be able to perform with style. This may be true but, in a competition, when she may be under stress or tired, her concentration lapses and she has to fall back on the *habit* which needs no conscious effort. Suddenly she is performing without style and losing marks.

If we always practise with quality of movement, and insist on good form, then the habits will be as valuable as the skills.

The message here is: always practise with good form and style, no matter how simple the element. If you don't, gradually you will develop bad habits which may not reveal themselves until an important competition brings them out under stress.

**Posture**

From the start we should try to develop good gymnastic posture or body position. We should educate the body into the straightest position possible. In Figure 6 a gymnast adopts two opposite body postures. Which one has the greatest height? Height gives energy. You will

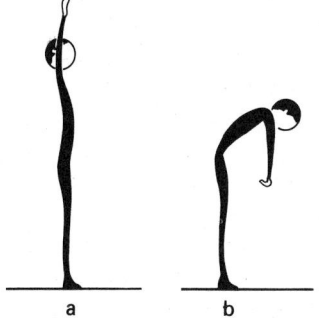

Figure 6     a       b

realize this if you compare falling out of a tree with falling off a chair. The greater the height, or the longer the body, the more *potential* energy that body has.

The straight body, fully extended, has good potential for movement; it also has fewer lever systems to burn up energy, and usually has greater aesthetic appeal.

**Basic elements on the floor**

By breaking down the basic elements on the floor into a genealogical tree it is possible to arrive at a basic vocabulary of moves.

Take the root elements:

1 Statics (balances)
2 Rolls
3 Overswings
4 Flights (somersaults),

and apply each to the following:

| *direction* | *shape* | *starting position* | *finishing position* |
| --- | --- | --- | --- |
| forwards | tucked | feet | feet |
| backwards | piked | hands | hands |
| sidewards | straddled | other body parts | other body parts |
| | straight | | |

You will see that for the rolls, for example, there are over 100 possible variations.

1 *The balances are:*
   the static position showing control, e.g. headstand, handstand, single leg scales, arabesques

2 *The overswings are basically:*
   the cartwheel – (sideways overswing)

the handspring – (forward overswing from one leg)
the flyspring – (forward overswing from two legs)
the back flip – (backward overswing)
the round-off – (centred side–back overswing)

3 *The flights are:*
the dives
the somersaults, with different degrees of rotation and
twists, in different body positions

The full vocabulary of elements can be found in the FIG
codes of points for men and women.

*Statics or balances*

The principles of balance are really quite simple and are
concerned with the following points:

1 *The base* – the part in contact with the floor and how
much area the base covers compared to the rest of the
shape. It is much easier to balance a pyramid on its
broad base than on its point. (Figure 7)

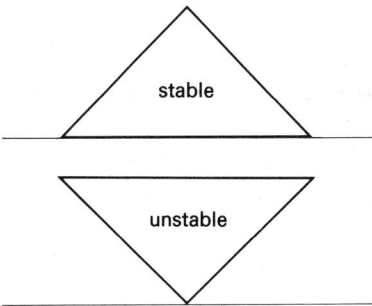

Figure 7

2 *The mass* – this is the shape and weight of the body and
it must be distributed evenly over the base for perfect
balance.

Taking the human body, the greater the area of body in contact with the ground and the more evenly the body's mass is distributed over the base, the easier the balance. It is also important to move into static position in a slow and controlled manner.

In Figure 8 compare the base of the arabesque and the straddle stand positions.

Figure 9  Static positions on the floor

Figure 8 *(right)* Arabesque and *(far right)* straddle stand positions

When balancing on small areas, as in single leg or arm balances, it is important to maximize the effectiveness of the base by ensuring even and overall contact with the floor of hands or feet. Spreading the fingers in the hand balances will make a slightly bigger base.

Some examples of statics on the floor are shown in Figure 9.

### The headstand

The headstand uses three points of support to make its base of balance. By using the hands and the head, a triangle is formed (Figure 10). You can see how the position of the head and hands will alter the size of the base triangle. Figure 10 d gives the best base area.

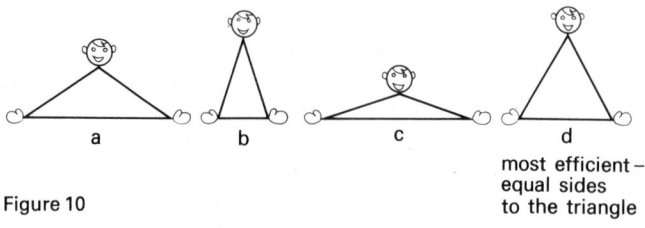

|   a   |   b   |   c   |   d   |

most efficient –
equal sides
to the triangle

Figure 10

*Physical prerequisites:* A good forward folding position is helpful, also sufficient strength in the arms and neck to support the body weight.

*Technical:* The headstand is achieved by the slow transition from a four point balance in the starting position, (Figure 11 a), to the three point balance at Figure 11 c. The base is gradually reduced as the feet are drawn towards the hands.

*Progressions:* Starting in the kneeling or crouching position, place the hands on the floor at shoulder width, with the fingers spread apart. Now place the *forehead* on the ground in front of the hands to form an equilateral

Figure 11 The headstand with bent leg lift

triangle. Gradually walk the feet towards the hands until the seat is above the head and you are almost able to move over to support on hands and head alone. By pressing on the hands and taking off one foot at a time, move to bent leg balance, (Figure 11 c). Now gradually extend to the straight position, keeping sufficient pressure on the hands to keep in balance.

This element can be performed close up to a wall in the first instances to encourage a straight back body position, not a hollow as in Figure 11 f. To come down, reverse the exercise slowly. This will help to increase control.

*Developments:* When the bent leg lift has been achieved, the move is made more pleasing by lifting with straight legs (Figure 12), first in straddle and then together.

The fast extension (Figures 11, c–e and 12, c–d) together with a thrust with the arms, will develop the headstand press to handstand and is a good strength exercise for headspring.

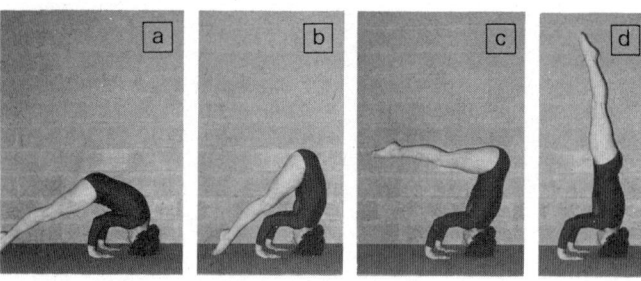

Figure 12   The headstand with straight leg lift

*Common faults:* Lifting to headstand then falling over the top is the most common problem and this is usually caused by: moving the hands back towards the head whilst lifting; transferring the weight from forehead to the top of the head; or trying to kick up too fast rather than lifting slowly.

Failure to reach the headstand position usually results from lifting the feet off before the hips are right over the head.

### The handstand

Gymnasts spend nearly as much time on their hands as on their feet, and the handstand is essential to the development of the other apparatus work. It is therefore abso-

Figure 13   The kick to handstand

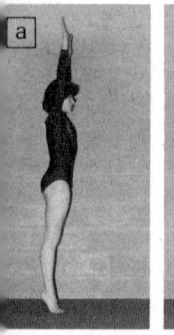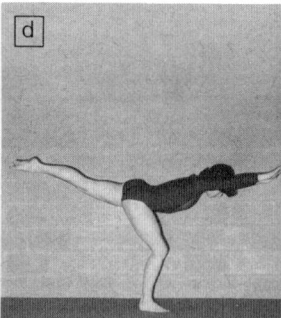

lutely essential that we master this most important of basic balances.

Handstands are arrived at in many different ways, but the main techniques are:

1 Kicking or swinging, in which the whole body swings to handstand assisted by a thrust from one leg.
2 The lifts, in which range of movement allows the body mass to be moved to handstand on straight arms with both legs being moved simultaneously.
3 The presses, in which more strength is employed to lift into handstand while extending the arms and shoulders.
4 The rolls – these are dealt with in the section on rolls.
5 The walkovers to and from handstand.

*The kick to handstand.*   This is most important for the development of handsprings and cartwheels, and the use of the wrong technique when learning to swing to handstand will have a decidedly adverse effect on all future developments.

*Prerequisites:* Good range of movement in forward and backward splits is essential, together with full shoulder extension. Strong arm and shoulder support in the handstand position and body tension are important.

*Technical* (Figure 13): From a fully extended standing position (a) the body rotates forwards and the front leg

steps into the lunge (c); keeping straight from hands to toes, the whole body rotates at the hips as the front leg lifts the hips by thrusting evenly (d), until the hands contact the floor at (f). The whole body now rotates about the hands at the wrist joint and is brought into a balanced state by the final extension of the front leg and the ankle joint. Having achieved the single leg balance first, the front leg is now swung up to handstand.

Important points are that the first leg controls the lift, while the body and back leg swing as one unit, keeping straight all the time.

*Progressions:* From the extended standing position raise on to toes and fall forwards. Step forwards into a lunge position, making sure that the first foot is pointing forwards, or turned very slightly out (never in), that the back is straight and arms fully extended forwards.

Throughout the move the head will be in a neutral and comfortable position so that you are able to look along the arms but not so far back that there is any tendency to hollow the back.

Practice stepping into the lunge and holding the position, then thrusting with the front leg back to standing.

Having mastered a controlled lunge, practise swinging the back leg up and the body down, keeping straight from fingers to toes while pushing your front leg straight. Do not reach down for the floor, but allow the swing of your body to bring the hands in contact. As you contact with your hands at shoulder width, push out even harder in the shoulders, taking the body weight on your arms without relaxing them. Push with your front foot to transfer the balance on to your hands in a one leg handstand. Only when you have a steady balance on one leg should you try to bring the front leg up to join the back one.

To come down elegantly, reverse the exercise – this will also increase your control.

*Common faults:* Failure to reach a satisfactory balance is usually due to impatience because the gymnast rushes to get both legs up before a steady one leg balance position is achieved. Most gymnasts fail to realize how important the front leg push is and try to rely on an excessive back leg swing which is difficult to control. Poor range of movement in the hips causes the swinging back leg to pull the front leg off before it has finished pushing.

The hollow back handstand results from relaxing the extension at some stage, or from poor range of movement in the shoulders, or from bringing the front leg up to join the back leg too soon.

*Development:* Correct execution of this move is essential if a good handspring, cartwheel and walkover are to be developed.

*The lift to handstand* (elephant lift). *Technical* (Figure 14): The technique is similar to that used in the headstand, except that we are transferring gradually from a four point balance to a two point balance. The base is diminished as before by drawing the feet towards the hands.

*Prerequisites:* A really good forward straddle fold, good shoulder mobility, and strength in the lifting position, which will develop by attempting the move.

*Progressions:* First stand in upright straddled position, feet comfortably apart, arms extended in a line with the back. (Figure 14a)

Piking at the hips and moving the hips backwards, bend forwards to place the hands shoulder width apart, on the floor (c). Note that at this stage there is no angle between arms and shoulders. Now lean the shoulders forwards and rock forwards until the weight is transferred mostly to the straight arms (d). Keeping the weight over the hands, draw the feet towards the hands lifting the hips as high as possible (e). Gradually the critical point will be reached

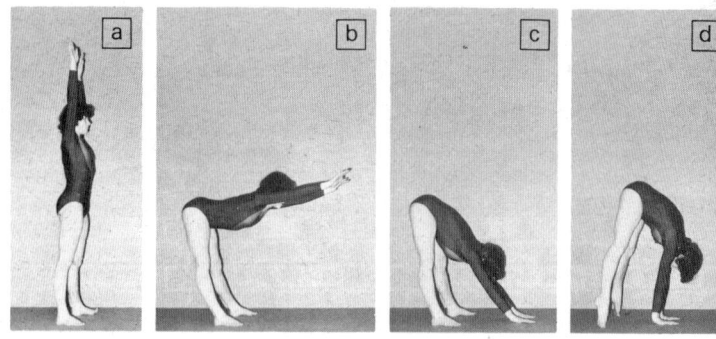

Figure 14   The elephant lift

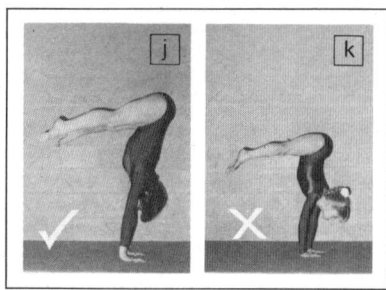

when the weight transfers to the arms only. At this point the legs are moved out to the side and lifted to handstand (f–i). Once mastered, lowering down in a controlled way should also be practised.

*Developments:* When mastered with the legs straddled, this lift is made more difficult by gradually bringing the

Figure 15   The elephant lift from a straddled half-lever starting position

 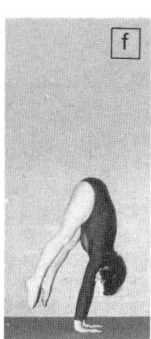 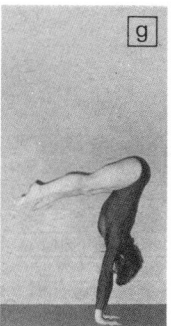  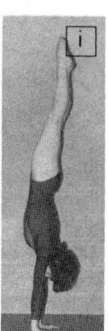

legs closer together until a piked lift is performed. Similarly, the lift is much harder from a straddled ½ lever starting position (Figure 15).

The lifts are an important development stage for work on the beam and bars, and really good elephant lifts will enable progress to be made more quickly to the more advanced skills.

This move should be practised daily. In the early stages it can be assisted by starting with the feet raised a little higher than the hands and by working up to a wall.

*Common faults:* The most common fault is related to the timing and many gymnasts experience great difficulty in performing the elephant lift because they try to lift the legs and feet before the hips are elevated fully above the head. If this happens, the lifting of the feet pushes the

  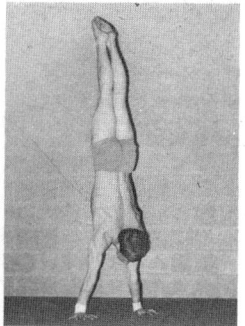

shoulders forwards and the gymnast compensates by hollowing the lower spine to bring the hips up (Figure 14 k).

This fault also appears when the gymnast is not strong enough at lifting in the shoulders. At all times the back remains rounded and the hips are elevated by opening the angle between arms and trunk. Basic weakness in this area is compensated for by hollowing the back to elevate the hips.

### The presses (Figure 16)

These are essentially like the lifts but instead of starting from a straight arm support, the starting position is with arms, or arms and legs, bent.

The press starts as the elephant lift but, when the body weight is transferred forwards, the arms bend. This makes it easier to elevate the hips over the hands (d). As the legs are raised the arms are progressively straightened.

*Common faults:* The most common faults with this element are the hollowing of the back, which must be avoided at all stages, and the failure to elevate the hips far enough over the head before the legs are raised.

This element may be practised with the hip close to a wall to give support, or with a partner.

Figure 16  A press

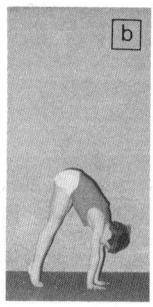

*The walkovers* (Figure 17)

This element is often included as an agility exercise, but the walkovers are in fact slowly changing balances from support on legs to hands to legs. They are performed forwards or backwards.

*Prerequisites:* These are the same for both forward and backward walkover: a very mobile spine, a really good splits with strength through the range, a full extension in the shoulders, a good support strength in handstand, and a good swing to handstand.

The mobility of the spine must be stressed again for this element since, unless the gymnast can execute a really good crab with the shoulders over the hands, further development will be difficult.

*Technical* (Figure 17): The forward walkover starts as for the handstand, but when the hands contact the floor the back leg continues to swing until a splits position is reached (g). At this point the front foot leaves the floor and the legs and hips rotate together at the hips until the back leg touches the floor (l) as close to the hands as possible. The arms thrust at this point to transfer the weight from arms to the back leg (m), and once balance is established the hands leave the floor and the trunk is raised to vertical (n) and the leg lowered.

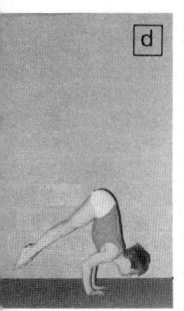   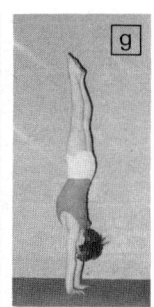

Figure 17   The forward walkover (a-n) and the backward walkover (n-a)

For the backward walkover read Figure 17 from right to left. This starts with a one leg balance with the other leg raised as high as possible (n). In a controlled way the trunk and extended arms are lowered backwards until the hands contact the floor (m). The weight is now transferred to the arms, the legs and hips rotate together in a straight line to g where the weight is transferred back to the front leg at f. Only when the balance is established on the front leg are the hands lifted off and the back leg lowered as from handstand (e–a).

The important point in the backward walkover is the bending back to support. During this stage the hips move forward to maintain balance. In a really controlled walkover, the gymnast should be able to stop at any point and either continue or return.

*Progressions:* There can be no substitute for really good preparation, particularly of the mobility of the spine and shoulders. This can be practised for forward and backward walkovers by using the wall and floor and gradually walking the feet or hands back down the wall trying to take as little support from the wall as possible. (Figure 18) Start with both feet together.

Figure 18a   Developing the walkover   Figure 18b

Always keep in balance and at no time fall backwards or forwards. When you can lower back to the floor with both feet straddled, gradually bring them together, then work from one leg. (Figure 18 a and b)

Patience and steady progress will enable you to master these elements properly.

*Development:* The walkovers are important elements on the beam, as well as the floor, and any faulty technique will soon be apparent on this apparatus. Free walkovers will later be helped by correct technique at this stage.

*Common faults:* Many girls find they can perform the walkovers sooner if they move fast through the element.

Figure 19

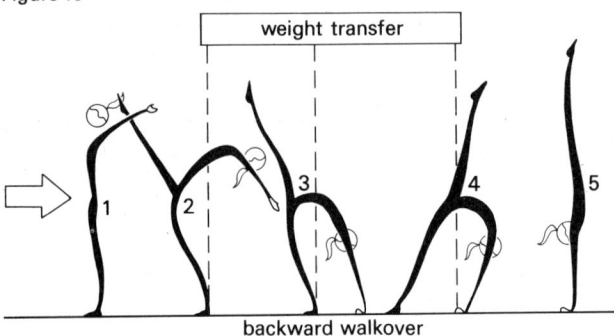

backward walkover

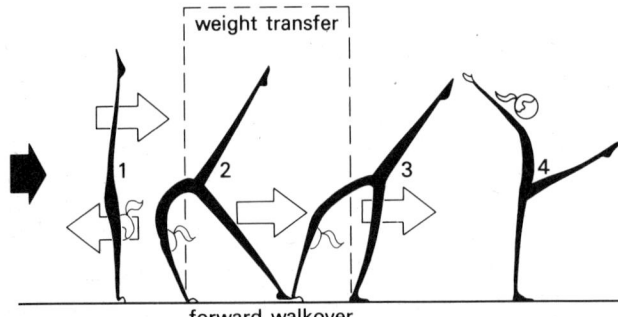

forward walkover

This is not recommended since it replaces correct technique. Learn the walkovers slowly before doing them fast.

The most common fault is falling back on to hands or legs rather than maintaining balance and lowering back slowly. You should be able to stop at any point in the move (Figure 19).

Falling back into walkovers puts unnecessary stress on the arms and shoulders and usually results in loss of control, particularly on the beam.

*Forward rolls*

The forward rolls are elements moving from different starting positions to different finishing positions, but involving a rotation of the body forwards while in contact with the floor.

Most common are the rolls from feet to feet or from handstand to feet in the tucked, straddled or piked positions. All the forward rolls have one part in common, that is the initial rotation using the shoulders as the axis. (Figure 20 e–g)

*Technical:* The starting positions of the forward rolls will always serve to bring the body to the extended position from shoulders to feet (Figure 20 e and Figure 25 c); from this position, the whole extended body rotates 40 or 50 degrees before the rotation is speeded up.

All rotations can be speeded up by shortening the length of the rotating body and in the forward rolls this is done by either tucking (Figure 20), piking and straddling (Figure 26), or simply by piking (Figures 27 and 28). It is important that the extended body starts to rotate before the tuck or straddle is started and for maximum effect this action should be left as late as possible. If the tuck position is maintained the gymnast would continue to roll forwards so, once the weight comes on to the feet (Figure

Figure 20   Tucked forward roll

20 i), the legs are straightened, thereby extending the rotating body and slowing the rotation to stand.

*Prerequisites:* A good straddle forward fold and a good forward pike.

These become increasingly important when moving on from the tucked forward roll to straddle and piked rolls.

*Progressions:* The forward roll tucked is the basic element and this can be split into two parts – each one learnt separately before combining.

Figure 21a

Figure 21b

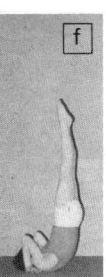 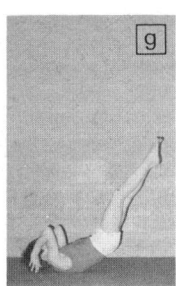   

Starting in the crouch position (Figure 20 a), reach forward and place the hands shoulder width apart on the ground in front. Now extend the legs and push with the feet until fully stretched, lifting the hips and keeping the arms straight. Keeping the extended position, bend the arms and tuck the head underneath until resting on the neck and shoulders with the feet still on the ground. Finally, extend the hips raising the feet behind until in a layout position on the shoulders as in Figure 20 e.

From this extended shoulder support the whole body rotates by pressing towards the floor with the feet until the last possible moment when the knees are drawn into the tucked position.

This part can be practised separately. First, by rocking on the shoulders and back (Figure 21 a) and gradually extending more and more (Figure 21 b). Other practices for rolling to feet are shown in Figures 22, 23 and 24.

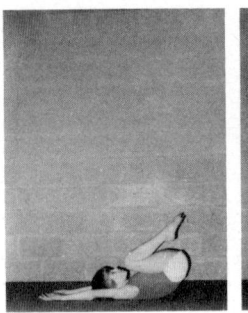

Figure 22   Practice for rolling to feet

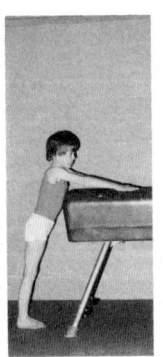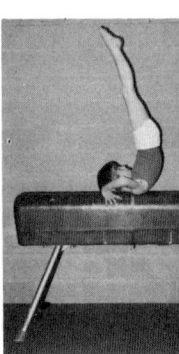

Figure 23   Practice for rolling to feet

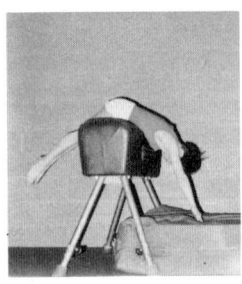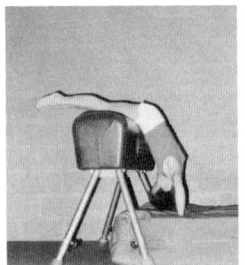

Figure 24   Practice for rolling to feet

 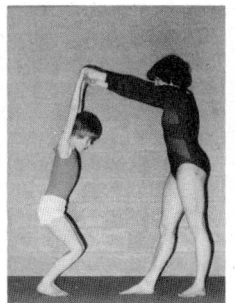 

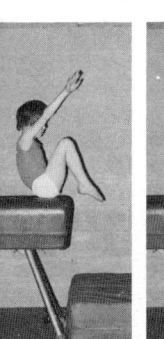 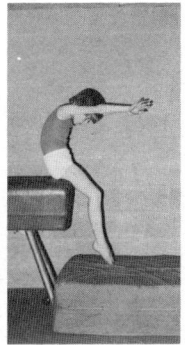  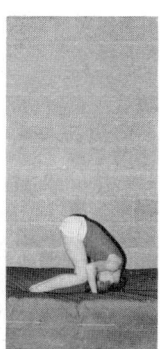

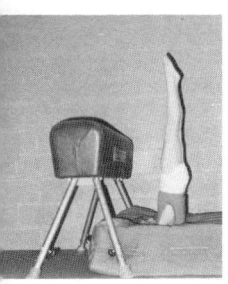

Figure 25   A straddle forward roll

Figure 26   A straddle forward roll

The straddle rolls and piked rolls are developed from this, since the initial stage of arriving at extended shoulder support is the same as for the tucked roll.

At the point when the gymnast would tuck in a tucked roll, the legs are straddled and the gymnast reaches forwards into a pike and pushes hard on the floor between the legs (Figures 25 and 26).

It is important not to try to sit up too soon before the rotation is completed and complete balance on the feet is felt.

By gradually bringing the legs closer together in the straddle roll, the full piked roll will develop until eventually there is no room to thrust between the legs and the hands must now be placed in the same relative position outside the legs (Figure 27 c). In this move it is more important than ever to maintain the pike position until the roll is completed back to feet.

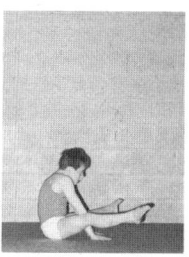

An inclined box top, or springboard with some mats on top, can help with the development of this move (Figure 28), but really good range of movement in the piked position is the secret.

*Progressions:* The straddle roll can be easily taken into any of the splits positions, simply by opening the legs wider and turning the hips. The roll from handstand is really only a handstand followed by a lowering into the extended shoulder support (Figure 29). This can be done by bending the arms, or by leaning forward on straight arms until the head tucks underneath. From there the move is the same as for the other rolls and can be performed tucked, piked or straddled, etc.

The dive rolls are a more dynamic development of the basic rolls involving a flight in which both hands and feet are off the ground at the same time for a short period.

The dive rolls are best learnt by gradually increasing the distance between the feet and hands at the start and by placing small obstacles to extend over. Rolled up agility mats are ideal, and a crash mat to land on is necessary initially. Gradually, the obstacles can be made higher (Figure 24), but always pad well with mats in the learning stages.

*Common faults:* Nearly all beginner gymnasts make the mistake of allowing the hip to drop to the floor from the shoulder support stage before extending the hips and

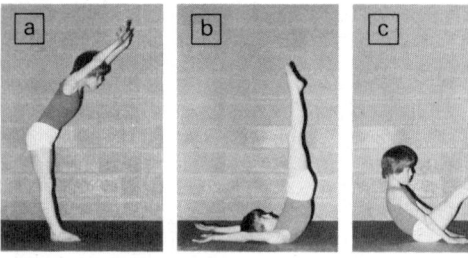

Figure 27   A piked forward roll

Figure 28   Practice for maintaining pike position until roll to feet is complete

Figure 29   The roll from handstand

Figure 30   Backward roll to handstand

allowing the rotation to develop. Remember the longer the body, the more *potential*.

Extending too early from the straddle or pike rolls causes the gymnast to sit back partially. Keep folded until securely in balance.

### Backward rolls

The backward rolls are really the forward rolls in reverse. They have the same developments, and can be performed with a tuck, straddle or piked shape.

The backward roll to handstand (Figure 30) is the final

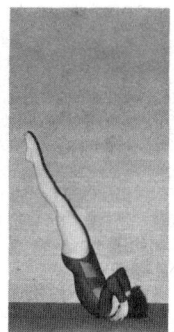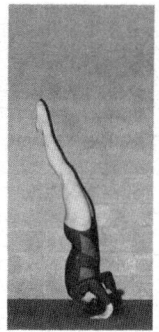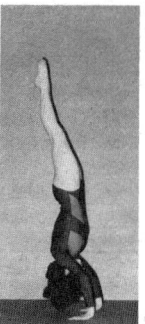

objective and, when properly performed to a held hand-stand, it is one of the most pleasing elements to watch and perform.

*Prerequisites:* As for the forward rolls, a good forward fold in straddle and pike is needed for the backward rolls to feet. For the backward roll to handstand, arm and shoulder strength is needed as in the headstand push to handstand.

*Technical:* In the backward rolls, a rotation is started from an extended standing position; this is accelerated by tucking or piking and is slowed down again by extending to feet or handstand.

In the backward roll to handstand the critical moment is when the extension of the body and the arm thrust occurs, since this determines whether the roll fails to reach handstand, arrives in handstand, or goes over the top. Only by trial and error can the optimum point of extension be found for the individual.

*Progressions:* The simple roll backwards may be a little unnerving at first and may be practised from sitting or crouching as in Figure 31. Here the hands are placed behind the head on the neck with the elbows pushed out and back. This protects the head from being thrown back. The knees are then brought over the top and to the floor

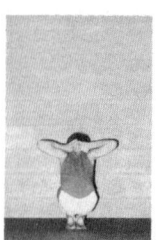   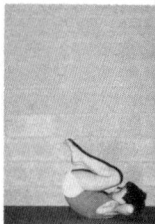

Figure 31 Practising the initial roll backwards

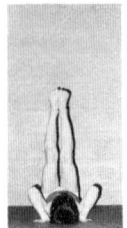    

Figure 32 Backward roll to feet

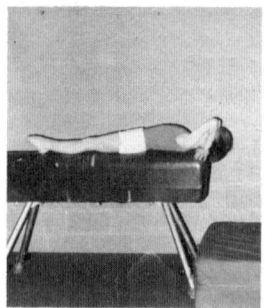   

Figure 33 Rolling back off a box top

as soon as possible. Gradually, as more experience is gained, the roll is brought to feet and the hands are placed back under the shoulders (Figure 32).

Once the basic backward roll from feet to feet is mastered in the tuck position, the finish may be performed with a pike or straddle. It is always important to bring the

feet directly over to the floor without extending the legs and hips as for the rolls to handstand.

Rolling back off a box top (Figure 33) may help to give awareness. When developing the roll backwards with straight legs, it is necessary to allow the shoulder and arms to swing backwards as the hips move back. This keeps a balanced state and avoids jarring the base of the spine (Figure 30 b–e).

*Developments:* The most important development is the backward roll to handstand. This is practised by sitting and rolling backwards to shoulder balance while quickly bringing the hands back under the shoulders to thrust with the arms.

Gradually, as the roll back to shoulders develops, try to thrust a little sooner with the arms each time, thereby lifting the shoulders off the ground. Each time push as hard as possible, but avoid rolling back over the top; when you have straightened the arms as much as possible you will have to tuck the head in and roll down again (Figure 35). Support from the coach will help the first committed attempt at pushing to handstand (Figure 34).

*Common faults:* Most backward rolls to handstand fail to stop in handstand, but move over the top of the balance point. This is usually due to failure to get the hands back fast enough under the shoulders; or placing the hands too close underneath the shoulders (the faster the backward roll the further back the hands reach until eventually the move can be performed with straight arms, as in Figure 36). Bringing the feet over the head towards the ground in a partial pike before thrusting with the arms produces a

Figure 34                    Figure 36

Figure 35    The push to handstand

Figure 37    The cartwheel

movement which is a piked backward roll followed by a beat to handstand, not as it should be – a true backward roll into handstand.

*Cartwheels or sideways overswings* (Figure 37)

Most gymnasts learn a cartwheel by copying without ever consciously learning the move. The cartwheel is, however, one of the most difficult moves to teach by breaking down into different stages.

Good preparation is essential as for all skills, but a mental picture of this element can help. The name 'cartwheel' describes very accurately what happens, for the arms and legs describe the same motions as would the spokes of a wheel. Often the cartwheel is learned from a forward start, which is incorrect as the true cartwheel is a sideways overswing. When trying the cartwheel imagine performing between two sheets of glass, which would only allow you to move in the one sideways plane.

*Prerequisites:* Good extensions in the shoulders, good side splits or box splits, good support in handstand, and the kick to handstand should have been mastered first.

*Technical:* The cartwheel is exactly like the kick to handstand with one leg only, performed by bending sideways.

First a sideways swing into straddle handstand, followed by a lowering down on the other side. The weight of the body is taken on the leading leg, then transferred to the leading arm, then to the second arm, then to back leg and finally back to both feet. Because there is a rapid transfer

Figure 38

Figure 39  The round-off or Arab spring

of balance, the body weight is distributed quickly as the spokes of a wheel distribute their load as the wheel rotates.

*Progressions:* The cartwheel may be learned by the following steps:

1   Kick into a one leg handstand, then change the position of the legs, i.e. lower the raised leg and raise the lowered leg up to handstand; come back to standing.

2   Perform this exercise and, at the same time, move one hand a little bit in front of the other. (If you swing your left leg up to handstand, move the left hand in front of the other.)

3   Gradually move the hand a little further each time until a full 180 degree turn is achieved.

4   This is effectively a cartwheel, but the starting and finishing positions are forwards, not sideways. Now try to swing to handstand sideways, a little more each time. Similarly, as you lower down from the cartwheel, try to keep in the same sideways plane.

5   Practise the whole move near to a wall, or on a line on the floor, and always keep the arms and shoulders extended in support.

6   When supporting, the coach should stand behind the performer and support the hips (Figure 38).

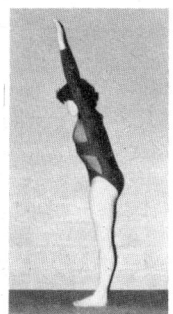

*Developments:* The cartwheel is the basis for the development of the 'round-off', the free cartwheel and the dive cartwheel, besides being a medium difficulty move when performed on the beam.

*Common faults:* There may be a lack of extension in the trunk and back causing a hollow backed cartwheel.

The most common fault of all is the cartwheel in which the legs do not pass over the hands in a direct line, but come round the side. (Both these may be corrected by returning to the cartwheel close to the wall exercise and the swing to handstand with straight body practice.)

The arms are sometimes not kept extended above the head when coming back to feet. This results in poor potential for any following moves and also looks untidy.

## *The round-off or Arab spring* (Figure 39)

The round-off is a direct development from the cartwheel and is the move that enables forward movement to be changed to backward movement. Although somersaults may be performed directly from the round-off, this move is usually used in a tumbling run to form the transition from forwards running to back flips.

*Technical:* This move can be thought of as a cartwheel that changes into a back flip. The move starts as for a cartwheel except that it is approached forwards and not sideways; also the hands are closer together and brought round the shoulder so as to be in a good position to thrust, in the same way as a ball is passed with the fingers of both hands pointing in towards each other. Try passing a ball with the fingers outwards.

As the second hand contacts the floor the legs are almost together and the thrust from hands back to feet is the same as the corresponding phase in the back flip.

*Progressions:*

1 Perform a cartwheel from a forward approach.
2 As 1, but finish facing the way you have come.
3 Now emphasize the thrust from the hands, but still keep the legs apart as in the cartwheel.
4 Finally, try to make the second leg catch the first. Do not stall the swing of the first leg to await the other catching up, as this will result in the move stopping in handstand at the top, and a pike down instead of a flight from hands back to feet.
5 Practise the last phase as in Figures 40 and 41, trying always to avoid piking too much.

The move should be learnt from a standing start and only used with a run or skip when completely mastered. Develop a good flat foot landing ready for the back flip (Figure 42).

Do not develop the bounce at this stage as this technique is only suitable for jumping somersaults, not for back flips and is very different (Figure 43).

*Developments:* The back flip follows on in a natural progression from the round-off, but the free cartwheel will also depend on the proper execution of this element.

Nearly all backward tumbles start with the round-off and then a badly executed start will upset the whole tumble.

*Common faults:* The first leg may be allowed to wait for the second to catch up. This can be corrected by practising the cartwheel action again. The hands may not be placed in such a way that they can push hard, i.e. fingers inwards. (The arms flex slightly to help the thrust from hands.) Another fault is piking down at the end instead of a flight from hands back to feet. Piking leaves the body in a poor position for subsequent back flips.

Figure 40

Figure 41

Figure 42

Figure 43

*Handsprings* (Figure 44)

The handspring is basically a kick through handstand performed very fast with an exceptionally strong thrust from the front leg so as to produce a flight from hands back to feet. The handspring can be performed to a one or two leg landing, but the handspring to one leg should be learnt first and practised from a standing start. A running handspring may bring early success of a kind, but will usually result in incorrect techniques.

*Prerequisites:* A really good swing to handstand, with all the necessary prerequisites of this element, will have prepared the gymnast for the handspring.

Figure 44   The handspring to one leg

*Technical:* As in the handstand, this element moves through the lunge position when the back leg and the trunk rotate rapidly at the hips (Figure 45(1)) while the front leg extends strongly. Good splits are necessary so that the front leg can continue to thrust all the time the back leg is swinging. The final thrust from the front leg is given by extending the ankle joint and pushing from the toes.

At the moment the hands hit the floor, all the forces should be acting together; rotation, given by the swinging back leg; height, given by the thrusting back leg acting through the hips; and extension and thrust given through the body by the thrust from the extended arms and shoulders.

to two legs

Figure 45 (1)

Figure 45 (2)  Incorrect technique

As the hands touch the whole body is tensed so that a bounce effect is achieved.

*Progressions:*

1  A really fast swing to handstand with one leg; practise up to a wall and keep the legs in wide splits.

2  The handstand bounce; swing hard into a handstand with one leg but, before going over the top, tense the body and thrust from the hands at the same instant they contact, reaching forwards; try to 'bounce' forwards several inches.

3  Combine the hard back leg swing with the bounce from hands. This is best done with the coach supporting (Figure 46), or from a raised platform on to crash mats.

4  Gradually, as the co-ordination is mastered, the gymnast will need less and less support. The handspring can now be attempted from a springboard covered with a mat (Figure 47) and finally at floor level only.

5 Once the handspring to one leg has been mastered (Figure 44), the handspring to two legs is very easy (Figure 44). This move is performed exactly as the handspring to one leg but, as the hands leave the floor, the back leg is swung to catch up with the first leg.

*Developments:* A good handspring will greatly assist the development of the free walkover and will lead on to tumbling progressions of handspring to one leg, followed by handspring to two legs, or handspring to two legs, front somersault.

*Common faults:* When swinging into the move, the front leg may not step out far enough under the hips, so that the thrust is directed more forwards than upwards, resulting in a long low handspring. The thrusting front leg must be under the hips as in Figure 45(1) c.

When swinging into the move, the arms may move first, producing an angle in the shoulders (Figure 45(2)). This reduces the effect of the bounce from the hands. The trunk and arms should swing together as in the exercise shown in Figure 48.

A poor splits position causes the swinging back leg to pull the front leg from the ground before it has had a chance to thrust out fully, resulting in a low handspring, often finishing in crouch.

Figure 46

Figure 47

Figure 48

### *Headsprings* (Figure 49)

The headspring is an element which seems to be temporarily out of fashion in women's gymnastics, but when performed to a splits or straddle fold can be most attractive. In men's gymnastics, the headspring front somersault is a most difficult element.

*Prerequisites:* A good understanding of the headstand (Figure 50), and a strong headstand to handstand press.

*Technical:* The headspring is really an overbalanced headstand/handstand thrust, performed best from piked to straight position. It relies to a great extent on a strong

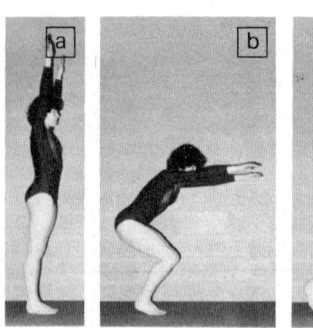

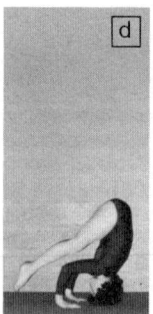
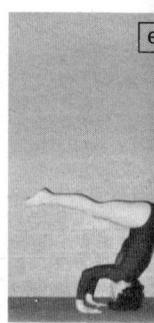

Figure 49   The headspring

Figure 50   The headstand

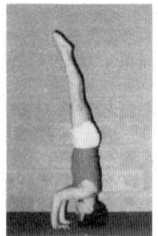
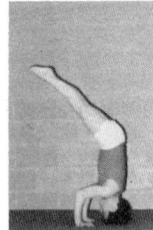

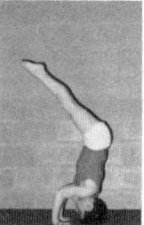
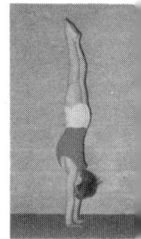

Figure 52

thrust from the arms, co-ordinated with the leg extension at the hips.

The direction of the headspring is given by the position of the hips relative to the hands at the moment the thrust starts. A line drawn through hands and hips gives this direction (Figure 51).

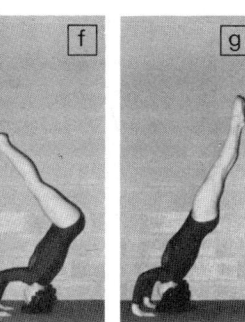

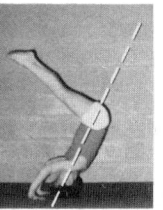

Figure 51

Since the headspring shows only the most momentary balance, it is not necessary for the head to be placed very much in front of the hands. What is most important is that the hips move out of balance (Figure 49 f) before the thrust takes place.

*Progressions:*

1  Start by holding a piked headstand position and beating and thrusting to handstand (Figure 52); this will develop the necessary arm and shoulder strength.

2  On a long box top at chest height, from the headstand in piked position, allow the hips to move over the top out of balance and beat and thrust as if going to handstand, but keep the feet moving over the top to the floor (Figure 53).Use a partner, or medicine ball, to practise a strong arm thrust as in Figure 54.

Figure 53

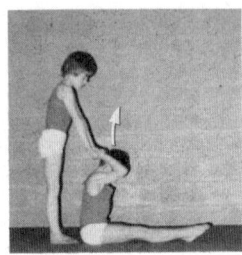

Figure 54

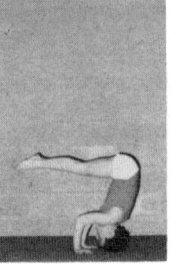
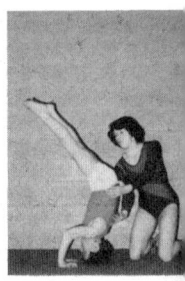

Figure 55

3   Gradually reduce the height of the box until the last section. At this point a pile of mats can be used and gradually reduced in height.

4   Try the headspring on to floor mats with a coach supporting (Figure 55).

*Developments:* The headspring is a fairly limited move, but is useful in the development of arm and shoulder strength. The headspring to one leg is a more difficult variation and the headspring to splits or forward fold can be used as linking movements.

*Common faults:* Failure to allow the hips to overbalance causes the high headspring to come down hard on the back.

### Back flips or flik flak (Figure 56)

The flik flak is a move which can be performed in series as a means of gaining backwards speed in preparation for jumps, somersaults etc., e.g. round-off back flip(s), back salto; or on its own as an individual skill e.g. on the beam, back flip to one leg or both legs.

The landing may be to one or both feet and the support may be to one or both arms, providing several variations to the basic move. Back flips on the beam require a slightly different technique and will be dealt with separately. Initially, the development is the same and should be learnt as an individual skill in its basic form to avoid the development of bad habits.

*Prerequisites:* As with all other gymnastic elements, successful acquisition of this skill is dependant upon the sound preparation of the body in the specific areas of strength, stamina and mobility. It is useful to have good range of movement in the back, lumbar region, the shoulders and ankles, whilst being able to maintain and

Figure 56   The back flip

control body tension. The arms and shoulders must be sufficiently strong to receive the weight of the body through handstand and to extend at the right time to produce the thrust back to feet; the legs must be strong enough to provide the initial thrust in the backward dive to handstand. The specific exercises from the general preparation programme are advised.

*Technical:* Whether as an individual skill, or in connected moves, the back flip, as its name indicates, involves a propulsion backwards, and for this at the point of thrust the centre of gravity of the mass of the body must be behind the feet (Figure 56c). To enable the legs to supply the thrust the body moves backwards in a straight position and rotates about the feet whilst flexion of the knee and hips occurs (Figure 56a–c). This backward rotation of the body is achieved initially in a straight body position whether from a standing position or from a preceding round-off, cartwheel, etc. The degree of distance achieved in the back flip will depend on the amount of body rotation before the leg thrust occurs at Figure 56d–f where it should be noticed the feet are flat to the floor although a final thrust comes from the extension of the ankle joint.

Figure 57

Figure 58

Figure 59

The move is then essentially a backward dive into handstand (g), where by rapidly extending the body and thrusting from the arms, the hollow handstand position is reversed to a dished position of the body during the flight back to feet, arriving back in the upright position ready to repeat.

In the case of the back flip leading to a somersault, the landing point is further away from the centre of gravity and on toes to facilitate the conversion of the horizontal velocity into vertical velocity.

*Progressions:*

1   For all beginners it is important to develop an awareness of moving backwards. The exercise shown in Figure 57 allows the gymnast to move backwards safely and also to take the body weight on the hands.

2   Partner activities to develop body tension through the initial rotation in a straight body position as shown in Figure 58.

3   Following from 2 the gymnast moves backwards into the sitting position with the hips behind the feet, back erect (Figure 59).

4   Another suitable partner activity for class teaching is shown in Figure 60. It is important that the supporting gymnast bends forwards in co-ordination with the backward fall of the partner.

5   Similar to Figure 60 but, by extension of the supporter's legs, additional momentum is given to the hips of the gymnast performing the flip (Figure 61).

6   The coach takes the gymnast slowly through the positions to familiarize him with the support which, initially, is under the shoulders and thighs, changing after the handstand to chest and thighs or shoulder and thighs (Figure 62).

7    The coach stands in whilst the gymnast develops the thrust to handstand position. It is not advisable for the gymnast to pike down to the floor after handstand, but to thrust away to land flat on a crash mat, or be supported by a coach (Figure 63).

8    The gymnast can hold wall bars and push away to develop strong backward thrusts, leading with the hands, arms and torso (Figure 64).

This element may be thought of in three phases: the movement backwards into the squat position ready to thrust, the thrust from legs and flight to handstand, and the extension and thrust from the arms and flight back to feet. Each of these may be taught separately and, as soon as possible, without support. For example the backward thrust to handstand can be practised from a solid base on to crash mats, and the thrust from hands back to feet using a box top or piled mats to give elevation to the body in relation to the ground (Figures 40 and 41).

*Development:* The development of this element will depend on the accurate execution of the individual stages and at all times emphasis should be placed on practising with good form. The correct starting postures and finishing positions are very important. It is inadvisable to teach this move from a round-off or a run until it has been completely mastered from a stationary position. Although a run or skip into round-off, followed by a back flip, will give more energy and make performance of a kind easier, the chances of taking short cuts in technique are greatly increased, and the gymnast is more likely to apply forces in the wrong way by assuming a position with the hips over the feet instead of behind the feet at take-off, by using the arms in a delayed swing, by performing jumps from the toes rather than thrusts from the legs. It is most important at all times to emphasize that the thrust occurs from flat feet although the ankle joint is extended at the end.

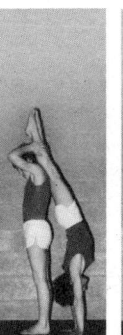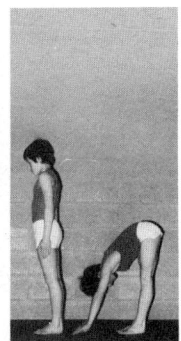

Figure 60

Figure 61

Figure 62

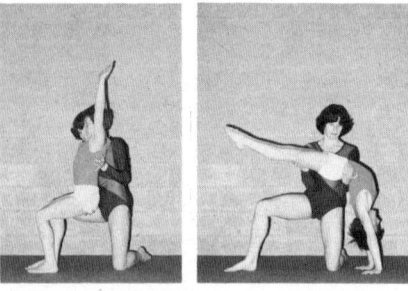

Figure 63

Figure 64

*Common faults:* The gymnast may perform very high back flips without covering any distance. This can be due to several factors. Check that the take-off is from flat feet and not from toes. A take-off from toes will usually indicate that the hips are not far enough back or that the gymnast is leaning forwards at the point of thrust. NB: A poor round-off will also have the effect of leaving the gymnast in a forward on-balance position if there has been no thrust from the arms.

The gymnast may have difficulty in passing through the handstand position without excessive bending of the arms. This can be due to a delayed arm swing. At all times the arms and hands should remain in line with the shoulders and hips so that the whole of this unit moves together, rather than the shoulders swinging backwards followed by a delayed swinging of the arms. Poor range of movement in the shoulders will increase this tendency, or insufficient support strength in handstand will produce an excessive bend of the arms.

# 3 Vaulting

Vaulting is probably one of the earliest sporting activities practised by mankind, developing from the time when an ability to leap over obstacles was a factor in the fight for primitive man's survival.

It is easy to see how this important survival skill could have developed into a competitive sport and how later, when man and horse became an inseparable team, that the horse should become a part of the game. Even today we have not become so far removed as to see no similarity between the streamlined wood and leather competition vaulting horse and man's companion and ally through the ages. The take-off area on the horse in men's vaulting still relates to the corresponding part of a real horse, i.e. neck and croup.

In the sport of Olympic gymnastics, the women vault from a cross positioned horse and the men from a long horse. In the case of the women, their vault scores contribute to a full quarter of their total marks and they have two vaults.

The men's vault carries one sixth of the total marks and they have only one chance.

I doubt if there are many gymnasts who spend a quarter or a sixth of their total training time working on the vault.

When looking at the FIG codes of points for men and women, there seems to be a confusingly large number of different vaults, but these all belong to one of two general groups – the hechts or the overswings.

In all vaults when the gymnast leaves the springboard, the body is rotating forwards, with the body's centre of gravity as the axis or centre of rotation, as in the dive forward roll (Figure 65).

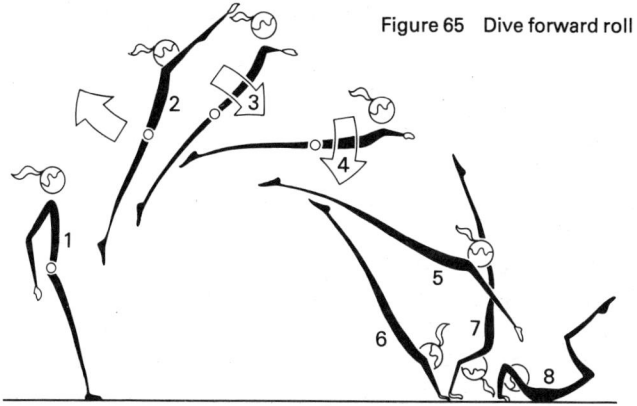

Figure 65   Dive forward roll

In hecht vaults, the initial rotation is fairly slow and the approach flight low so that, when the strike with the hands occurs, the direction of rotation is reversed (Figure 66). This reversed rotation can be speeded up further by tucking or straddling to give the squat or straddle vaults respectively.

Figure 66

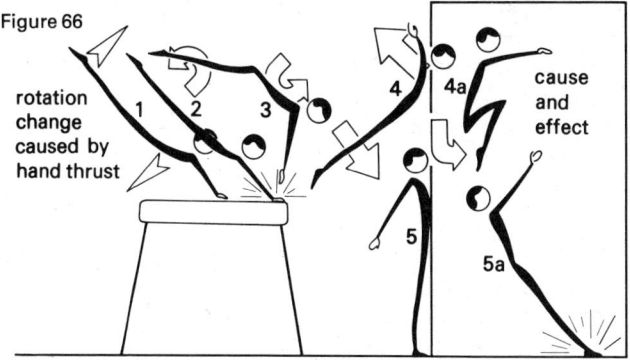

rotation
change
caused by
hand thrust

cause
and
effect

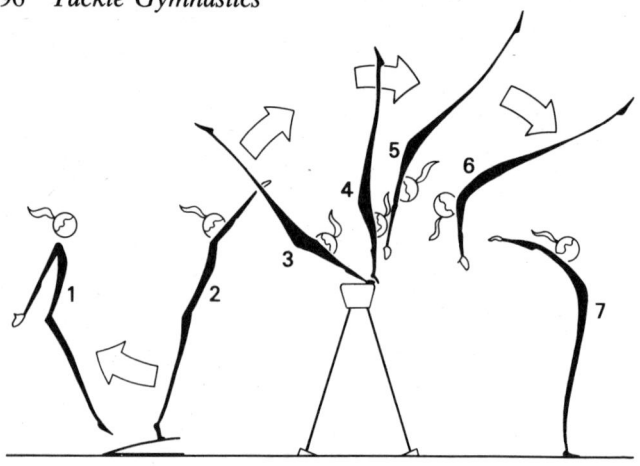

Figure 67   Straight arm overswing

In the overswing or long-arm vaults, the initial rotation is faster than for hechts and the approach flight higher so that, when the strike with hands occurs, the rotation continues in the same direction (Figure 67).

The hecht vaults, although basic to school gymnastics in the form of the squat, straddle and stoop (straight leg squat), seem to have fallen from fashion in most clubs, where even very young gymnasts start with the overswings. However, the more advanced straight body hecht with twists are as difficult as any overswings.

In this book, we shall only be looking at the very basic vaults and progressions but, as in the other chapters, the emphasis is on getting the basics perfect so that the more complex and difficult vaults may be better understood.

## Different phases of vaults

For a better understanding of the teaching progressions of the different vaults, it is convenient to look at the phases which all vaults have in common, as shown in Figure 68.

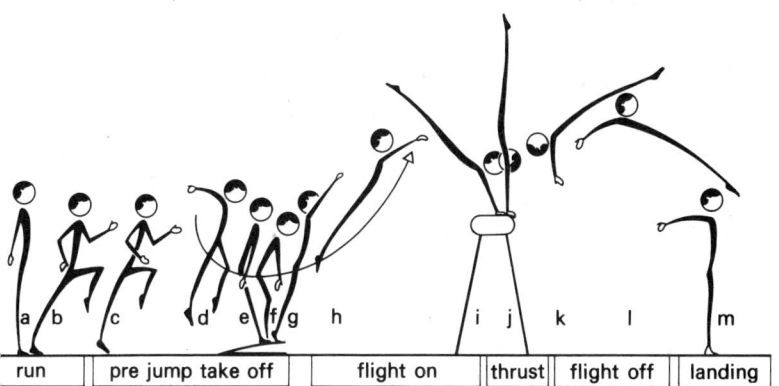

Figure 68

|   |   |
|---|---|
| a–c | the run-up |
| c–e | the hurdle step |
| e–g | the strike from the springboard |
| g–i | the first flight |
| i–j | the strike on the horse |
| j–m | the second flight |
| m | the landing |

*The run-up* (Figure 68 a–c)

The run-up for the vault may be likened to the run-up for the long jump in athletics, the purpose being to develop as much horizontal velocity as possible. What self-respecting long jumper would consider competing without knowing exactly the length of run-up and the number of strides needed to reach the take-off board? Many young gymnasts, however, have never practised a measured run-up and every vault is a matter of trial and error with compensating steps or skips before take-off.

A well practised measured run-up will free the gymnast

from worry about getting to the board and allow maximum concentration on the vault. This will also allow the gymnast to watch the horse all the time during the run-up in preparation for the hand positioning, rather than the focus of attention being on the board and suddenly transferred to the horse at the last second.

When practising the measured run-up, it is important always to start with the same leg and to keep the strides even and of the same length while accelerating.

Run-ups cannot be practised at half speed so, to avoid extra complications at the beginning, the run-up and jump to the springboard need only be followed by a long jump or dive roll on to crash mats, without the horse. Only when the run-up is well established should the horse be introduced.

With younger children there should be no insistence on a set number of strides, but they must always start with the same leg and run at full speed until, by trial and error, an appropriate distance is found to give a successful contact with the springboard.

### The hurdle step (Figure 68 c–e)

This is the point where the gymnast finishes the last stride of the run-up and takes off from one foot to land on two feet on the springboard.

The hurdle step is very important, since it determines the point of landing on the springboard and the angle of the body at take-off.

The hurdle step should not be an exaggerated leap, but should fit in smoothly with the run-up, so that the forward speed is maintained.

During the hurdle step, the angle of the body at strike, and therefore the subsequent direction of the first flight, is determined.

*The strike* (Figure 68 e–g)

I like to think of the strike on the board as the first stage in a two stage rocket take-off, the second stage being from the horse. It is at the strike that all the energy of the run-up is converted into flight.

The legs and feet thrust vigorously into the board and then tense to receive the recoil of the springboard. The action is not of jumping, but of bouncing, and the whole body must be straight at the culmination of this phase.

Very simply, three factors influence the first flight: the speed of the run, the thrust by the legs at strike, and the angle of the body at strike. Figure 69 shows three different angles of strike and how the resultant flight direction varies. The forces $F_1$ for running speed and $F_2$ for strike thrust are assumed to be the same in this example and are proportional to the lengths of the sides of parallelograms. It can be seen that keeping the body leaning back at strike will cause a higher slower flight, while to lean forwards gives a fast low flight.

Only by many practices in a safe situation can the gymnast build up enough experience of the different combinations of the forces and their effect on the resulting

Figure 69

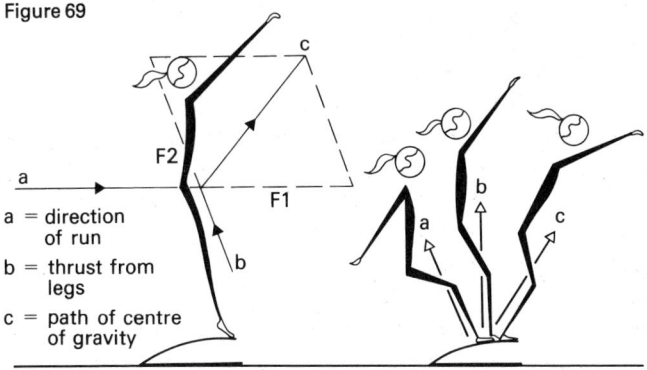

a = direction of run

b = thrust from legs

c = path of centre of gravity

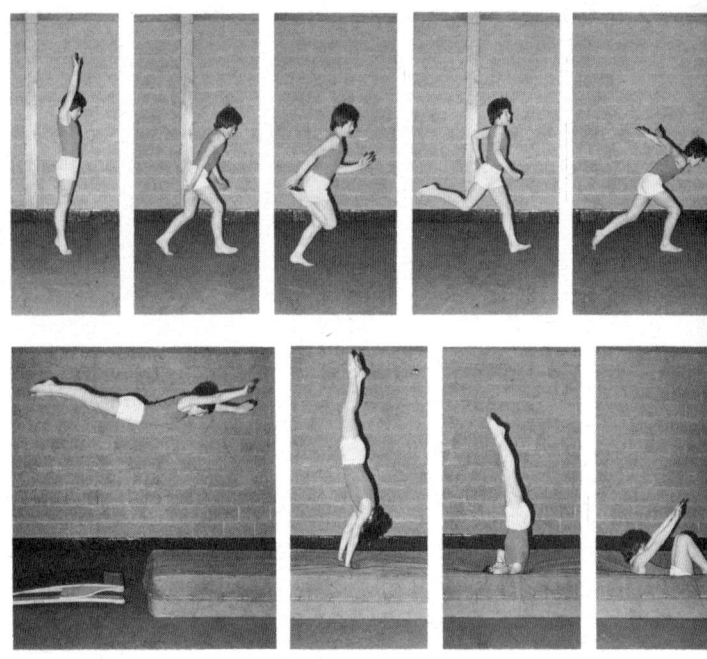

Figure 70   Practising the run-up, hurdle step and strike

flight. It is easy to see that if we can standardize the run-up speed and the thrust there are fewer variables than when every vault has a different approach speed etc.

Probably the best way of practising the run-up, hurdle step and strike, is that shown in Figure 70, where there is no concern about a vault and the experience of different flights can be gained from a vertical jump to the dive roll on to the safe landing crash mats. The more the better!

### *The first flight* (Figure 68 g–i)

The first flight from springboard to horse has to be long enough for the body to achieve a layout or straight and

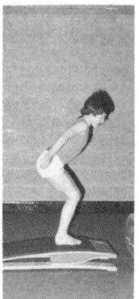

extended position and yet not so long as to allow the body to lose momentum.

Nowadays, the concept of the vault has changed so that the horse is not something to vault on to and then off, but acts as a second stage boost for the initial thrust from the springboard. The handspring vault then becomes more like a straight somersault in which extra height is gained from the contact with the horse. During the first flight the amount of rotation of the body determines whether the vault will be a hecht or overswing, but the arms are always swung forwards into a layout body position.

### The strike on the horse (Figure 68 i–j)

This is now likened to the second stage thrust which comes from the arms and shoulders, either to reverse the direction of rotation, as in hechts, or to augment the flight rotation, as in the overswings. At the point of strike the body must be in tension as for the handstand bounce practice for handsprings.

### The second flight (Figure 68 j–m)

This should show a lift from the horse, and during this phase the body completes rotation to allow the landing in the vertical position. The height and length of the second flight are entirely determined by the preceding phases and, once the hands leave the horse, the flight is determined and cannot be altered, even though the body positions can be changed.

### *The landing* (Figure 68 m)

The landing is also determined by the accuracy of the other phases, but control can be practised and many gymnasts get into the bad habit of not bothering about controlled landings during training.

In landing, the legs and body bend to absorb the force of the fall, until a point of balance is found when the body is straightened to a standing finish (Figure 71). The arms are also used to control balance by extending to the side.

### Squat and straddle vaults

The squat and straddle vaults are essentially the same vault, differing only in the body position in the second flight. In both vaults, the tuck or pike straddling of the legs occurs after the hands strike the horse, and serve to reduce the body's length so that the rotation is speeded up to allow the gymnast to land on his feet.

Both vaults can be learnt at the same time simply by alternating the second flight phase.

Start on a long horse or box and, from crouching, jump from feet to hands, keeping the shoulders forward, push off instantly with the arms and shoulders and tuck or straddle. A double thickness of crash mats will enable the coach to avoid the normal support of upper arms (Figure 73 a and b).

Gradually the gymnast will start further and further back on the single horse, until a layout position is

Figure 71   Landing

Figure 72   The handstand bounce practice

developed; this will be achieved at the gymnast's own speed as confidence grows. The handstand bounce practice (Figure 72) should be practised in conjunction with the vaults to develop a strong instant thrust of arms and shoulders and good body tension. Keep the handstand bounce long and low.

As the gymnast develops a longer layout, two boxes may be placed together as in Figures 74 and 78, until a stage is reached when a full extension of the body is being achieved confidently. This is the time to introduce the

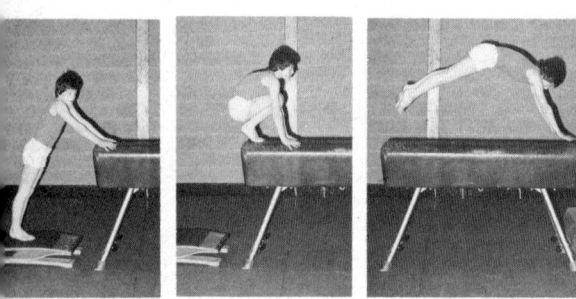

Figure 73a

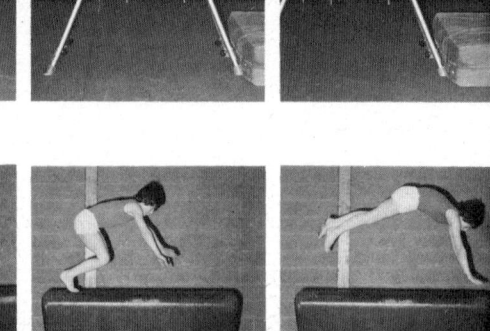

Figure 73b

Figure 74

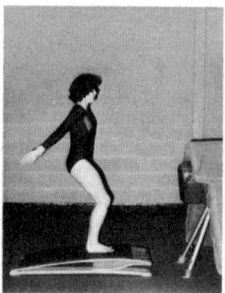

Figure 75

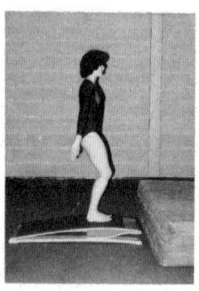

Figure 76

springboard; but, once a layout is achieved, never reduce the distance, simply use crash mats and boxes to keep a soft landing underneath, between springboard and horse (Figure 75). For the boys vaulting on long box, it is now only a short step to vaulting without a safety mat covering the horse, as confidence grows. For girls, gradually reduce the height of the boxes (Figure 75) between springboard and horse, keeping the crash mat on top until only the crash mat is at ground level (Figure 76) – eventually this mat can also be removed.

Using this method the layout distance remains constant and the springboard is never brought closer to the point of hand contact on the horse. In these vaults the main element of fear occurs when bridging the void between

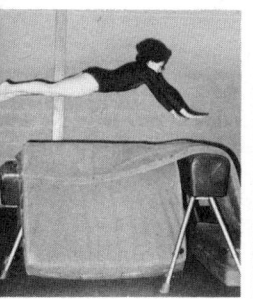   

springboard and horse and it is this fear that inhibits good layouts. There is no substitute for good crash mats, properly positioned; these allow the gymnast to work independently without the need for a supporting coach. Where standing in is necessary because of lack of equipment, the coach should stand at the side and support the upper arms, moving forward with the gymnast. Never support from the front – the gymnast will worry more about hitting the coach than about the vault.

### Handspring vaults or long arm overswings

The handspring is not a particularly good description of the long arm overswing vault because, unlike the handspring, both legs lift at the same time from the spring-

Figure 77

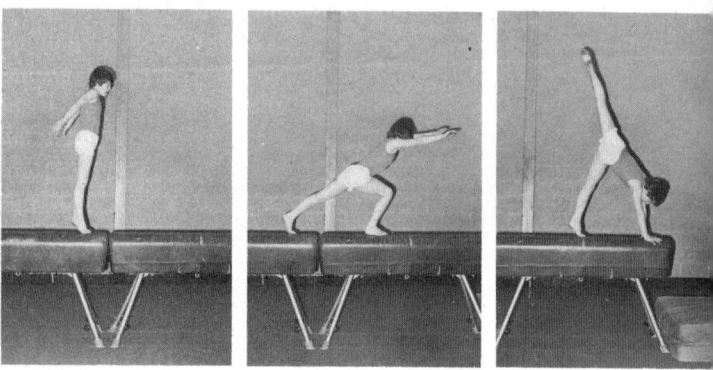

Figure 78

board. This vault should perhaps be named the flyspring but, whatever the name, this vault is the basis of the great majority of advanced vaults, and the correct mastery of this element will be an invaluable step towards the more difficult elements.

Before attempting to learn handspring vaults, a really good handspring from straight arms should be mastered on the floor, together with continuing practice of the handstand bounce (Figure 72).

When practising the handstand bounce for vaulting, the arms should be swung from behind forwards into the

extended body position, rather than from above the head.

To develop further the experience of flight, the high dive forward roll can be practised over a well protected box (Figure 77), until a straight front somersault develops (Figure 79).

Develop the handspring technique from the long box (Figure 78), following the same progressions as for the squat and straddle vaults.

As the vault is developed, great attention should be given to producing a straight body out-flight since this will facilitate the learning of overswings with twists. When

improving the
straight arm
overswing

Figure 79 Straight front somersault

practising all vaults it is important to give the utmost effort and to approach each time with the firm intention of completing the skill; a half-hearted run-up will only end in frustration.

For the coaches there is no substitute for an abundance of good quality crash mats for teaching vaults. The sooner the gymnast is freed from the psychological prop of the coach's presence the better, but the gymnast must be aware of the inherent dangers of vaulting and of how the crash mats can be used to inspire confidence.

The springboard is also of paramount importance; a really good Reuther board is required for competition vaults and it is advisable to inform the manufacturers when ordering of the age and ability of the gymnasts working, since older boys and girls can soon break a junior board. To minimize fatigue and allow greater numbers of repetitions with an exaggerated flight potential, the trampette can be a valuable teaching aid, but this apparatus is potentially very dangerous and should never be used except under the closest supervision of a qualified and experienced instructor.

# 4 The gymnast's programme

**Yearly programme**

The gymnast's yearly programme of work is decided by the competition season and changes accordingly. These dates may vary from year to year, but the principle is the same.

*November–May – competition season*
The gymnast is working on perfect whole routines and will have a set exercise and a voluntary exercise on each apparatus.

The aim is to have such familiarity with the exercises that the question asked on the day is not: will I get through my routines? But: how perfectly and with what expression will I get through my exercises?

The competition season is no time for trying new moves, or changing music.

*June and July*
This is the holiday period with a well earned rest from competitions – a time for the fun of summer displays and training to keep fit.

*August*
An intensive period of suppling, and building up strength and stamina, with many repetitions of basic skills.

The aim is to prepare an increased physical capacity for learning new elements.

*September*
Learning new elements for the routines, practising them individually.

*October*
Starting to put the new elements into the routines, and building up more elements together.

*November*
Full routines for the new competitive season.

## Weekly programme

The number of times a gymnast should train in one week is difficult to establish. It depends on the individual and how hard they work while in the gym.

The very young gymnast need only have one or two one hour sessions a week, building up to three or four two hour sessions.

Remember, though, that the effectiveness of the many sessions will depend on how much preparation the gymnast is doing at home. It is the preparation work which really determines how fast you can learn.

## Daily programme

In the daily training sessions, it is best to try to keep preparation work separate from skill learning, but every day a regular suppling programme should be followed. For example, get up half an hour earlier and have a hot bath, put on warm clothing and go through the suppling programme before breakfast. Regular, light sessions will have a much better effect than very strenuous, but intermittent, practices. Before bed each day do a few strengthening or conditioning exercises.

**The training session**

For the teacher and coach a sample lesson plan is included. For the beginner's classes nearly the whole of the lesson is devoted to preparation exercises, but these should be made as interesting as possible by including them in games, partner exercises and team competition.

As the gymnast progresses on to more advanced work and becomes fully aware of how to prepare the body, she will be expected more and more to take on the responsibility of keeping fit and in the right physical condition to make best use of the coach's time. With so little time available for training, the sooner the gymnast is able to take over personal preparation the sooner the coach can concentrate on teaching new skills.

During the competition season, the gymnasts will be practising routines in the skill sessions.

# Lesson plan

This plan is intended for a group of twenty-five gymnasts who have had some previous experience, i.e. they have been made aware of their responsibility with regard to range of movement and strength and are working a programme of development at home.

### Warm up

Warm up to heat the muscles need only be short (five minutes), providing the body is suitably insulated. Make sure the children have hats, gloves, socks, track suits.

Do rapid and dynamic exercises such as team games, partner activities, followed by more specific warm up related to the elements intended to be worked. Make this a fun period.

### Suppling/limbering up

More partner work directed towards range of movement. Bring the habit lengths of muscles out to full relaxation. Spend five minutes on this.

### Specific range

Five minutes range and strength exercises intended to be covered in the session, e.g., if you intend to work on back flips, spend five minutes on shoulder range, leg extension games and exercises.

**Group work or class teaching of main theme of lesson**

Recap on past work done on this theme. Lead into new work by demonstration or visual aids. Use whole/part whole system for teaching skills, i.e. show the whole thing then break it down into more easily learned parts; when completed try to put the skill together.

e.g. *Back flip*

Show the child an advanced performer doing the move. Take him/her through the total skill with full support. Separate the three parts for practice.

1 Crouch – and move off balance, feet flat, shoulders extended.
2 Thrust to handstand.
3 Straight thrust back to feet and crouch.

This phase can be taught as partner work, depending on the size of the group, or in threes or fours.

Relate the work to other moves and connect moves as soon as possible.

This pattern can be repeated on the different pieces worked. Keep the skill content short, since skills break down with fatigue.

Spend fifteen minutes on each element.

All the elements dealt with in this book are basic but important to good further development. The techniques explained are based on mechanics of movement and are, of course, subject to compromise as the coach has to try to adapt them to the individual. It has been our experience that the more compromises and short cuts taken at this stage, the more problems encountered later on and if you haven't already noticed our gentle hinting . . .

*Preparation makes for Perfection*